M.C. ESCHER™

Works of Art

WINGS BOOKS
New York • Avenel, New Jersey

Copyright © 1994 by Random House Value Publishing, Inc.

All M.C. Escher illustrations:
© 1994 M.C. Escher/Cordon Art—Baarn—Holland. All rights reserved.

Grateful acknowledgment is made to the M.C. Escher Foundation in Baarn, Holland,
for permission to use their photographs of the artwork.

This 1994 edition is published by Wings Books,
distributed by Random House Value Publishing, Inc.,
40 Engelhard Avenue, Avenel, New Jersey 07001.

Random House
New York • Toronto • London • Sydney • Auckland

Printed and bound in Malaysia

Library of Congress Cataloging-in-Publication Data

Escher, M. C. (Maurits Cornelis), 1898–1972.
    M.C. Escher : works of art.
       p.   cm.
    Includes bibliographical references.
    ISBN 0-517-11925-0
    1. Escher, M. C. (Maurits Cornelis), 1898–1972—Catalogs.
I. Title.   II. Title: Works of art.
NE670.E75A4   1994
769.92—dc20   94-20418
                                                 CIP

8 7 6 5 4 3 2 1

"I can't stop fooling around with our irrefutable certainties. It is, for example, a pleasure knowingly to mix up two- and three-dimensionalities . . . to make fun of gravity. . . . Are you really sure that a floor can't also be a ceiling? Are you definitely convinced that you will be on a higher plane when you walk up a staircase? Is it a fact as far as you are concerned that half an egg isn't also half an empty shell?"[1]

—M. C. Escher

1. *Eight Heads*
   January, February or March 1922

2. *Procession in Crypt*
   July 1927

3. *Tower of Babel*
   February 1928

4. *Castrovalva*
   February 1930

5. *Atrani*
   August 1931

6. *Day and Night*
   February 1938

7. *Hand with Reflecting Sphere*
   January 1935

8. *Cycle*
   May 1938

9. *Sky and Water II*
   June 1938

10. *Fish*
    October 1941

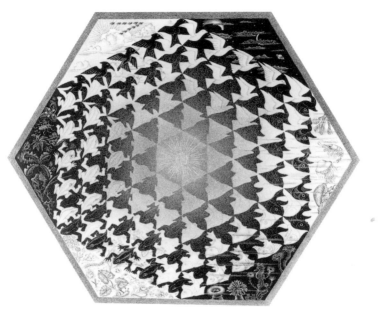

11. *Verbum (Earth, Sky and Water)*
     July 1942

12. *Encounter*
    May 1944

13. *Reptiles*
   March 1943

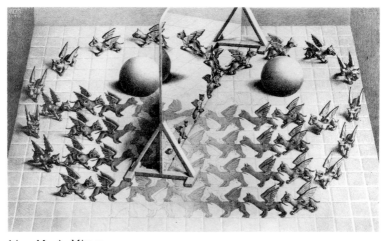

14. *Magic Mirror*
     January 1946

15. *Gallery*
    December 1946 (first state)—April 1949 (further states)

16. *High and Low*
    July 1947

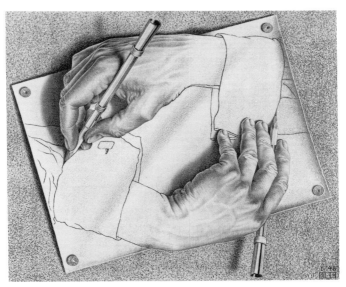

17. *Drawing Hands*
    January 1948

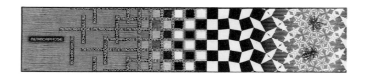

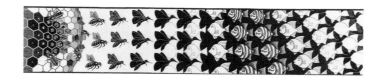

18. *Metamorphosis III*
    [I, II, III, IV]
    1967–68

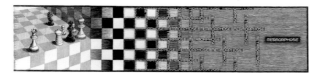

19. *Metamorphosis III*
    [V, VI, VII, VIII]
    1967–68

20. *Concentric Rinds*
     May 1953

21. *Order and Chaos*
    February 1950

22. *Presdestination*
January 1951

23. *Regular Division of the Plane with Birds*
     April 1949

24. *Tetrahedral Planetoid*
    April 1954

25. *House of Stairs*
     November 1951

26. *Depth*
October 1955

27. *Three Worlds*
    December 1955

28. *Print Gallery*
    May 1956

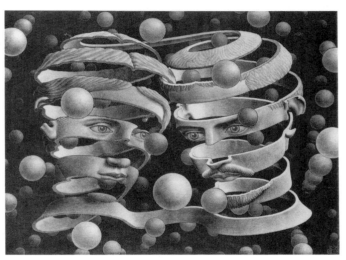

29. *Bond of Union*
     April 1956

30. *Regular Division of the Plane III*
June 1957

31. *Regular Division of the Plane V*
   June 1957

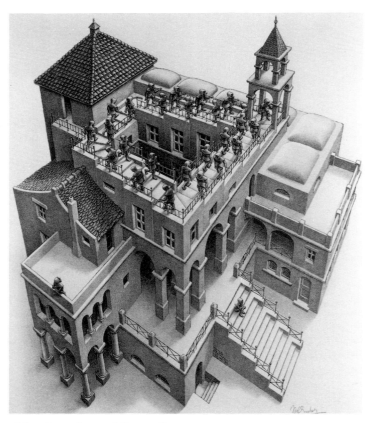

32. *Ascending and Descending*
    March 1960

Afterword

During an interview four years before his death, the celebrated Dutch graphic artist, M. C. Escher, characteristically summed up his chosen lifework with rueful playfulness: "I never really wanted to build houses. Only *mad*houses."[2] Having never pursued his parents' dream for him of a career in architecture, Escher turned his boyhood hobbies of drawing and woodworking into one of the most inspired and imaginative graphic art careers of the century.

Maurits Cornelis Escher, the youngest of five sons, was born June 17, 1898 into a family of scientists and engineers. Raised and schooled in Arnhem, Holland, he displayed little aptitude for mathematics or science, though he would later attribute his affinity for the "mathematical" and his methodical work habits to the "scientic milieu" in which he grew up.[3] What Escher loved as a boy were his lessons in woodworking with a carpenter's apprentice, listening to and playing classical music with friends, and above all else, drawing.

Escher was producing his first simple linocuts (designs cut into a block of linoleum) and creating prints from the cuts as early as 1916. These came to the attention of renowned Dutch graphic artist R. N. Roland Holst who praised the young student's work and later urged Escher to start making woodcuts. His first engravings in wood were simple, single-motif designs and he immediately took to the new process: "It is splendid work, but much more difficult than working in linoleum. . . ."[4]

In 1919, as a first-year student at Haarlem's School for Architecture and Design, Escher showed his designs to graphic artist and teacher, Samuel Jessurun de Mesquita, who urged Escher to abandon his architectural studies and pursue the graphic arts full time.

Two years later, in 1922, Escher produced a series of 15 original woodcuts as illustrations for a friend's book. Two of these designs show Escher's growing interest in exploring the ideas of geometric symmetry and contrasting dualities. *Beautiful* is a series of compositionally balanced black and white triangular motifs designed around what became one of Escher's favorite graphical techniques: pure central symmetry. When the print is rotated 180° (turned upside down), the illustration is exactly the same. A second print, *The Scapegoat*, gives visual expression to another of Escher's recurrent themes: "philosophical duality." The perfectly balanced juxtaposition of life's eternal scapegoats—the devil and the saint, the dark and the light, forces seemingly separate but forever linked—is a direct predecessor of *Eight Heads* (plate 1), Escher's first design composed around the principle of regular division of the plane.[5] The heads of four men and four women are regularly repeated, with no space between the motifs. At first glance, the viewer only sees two conventional-looking men wearing hats and two women with elaborate hair styles. However, when the design is rotated 180°, the heads of two malevolent-looking men with beards appear with two different women.

From the early 1920s to the mid-1930s, Escher traveled extensively throughout southern Europe. There he met and married his wife, Jetta, began raising a family, and settled in Rome for eleven years, until the Nazi occupation forced him to leave in 1935. Escher was much taken with southern Italy's architecture and landscape and produced several free-style lithographs of the countryside. *Castrovalva* (plate 4), sketched during a trip through the Abruzzi mountains, and *Atrani* (plate 5), an overhead view of a site on the coast of Amalfi, are meticulously rendered landscapes, "faithful observations of reality." In contrast to *Atrani's* controlled view from above, *Tower of Babel* (plate 3), completed during the same period, utilizes a dizzying, extreme vantage point above the tower and is Escher's first experiment with "impossible" buildings and perspectives. In conventional pictures, one or more vanishing points are usually placed on the horizon. In *Tower of Babel*, the focus or vanishing point is the nadir, directly *below* the viewer's feet.[6]

It was during trips to Spain in the 1920s that Escher developed his lifelong affinity for geometric symmetry, plane-filling designs and regular division. He repeatedly visited the Alhambra palace, making numerous sketches based on the repeated decorative tile designs used on the palace's floors and walls. While he was impressed by their "great intricacy and geometric artistry," Escher also remarked on "the total absence of any human or animal form" and suggested that this was "perhaps both a strength and a weakness at the same time."[7] The latter remark was prophetic. When Escher began formalizing his theory on the regular division of the plane, two of its basic tenets would be that the motifs used in a repeated design must be clearly *recognizable* (preferably by using light-and-dark contrasts to insure the individuality of the motif), and be "living creatures" instead of "inanimate objects."

Escher's first regular division pattern of a single motif featured lions, but the artist came to prefer birds and fishes for their natural angularity and simple, easily reversible shapes.[8] The justification for this preference is ably demonstrated in the elegantly composed *Sky and Water I* (front cover) and *Sky and Water II* (plate 9). In these early explorations on the theme of metamorphosis, "the white fish silhouettes merge to form the 'sky' for the birds, while in the lower half the black birds blend together to form 'water' for the fishes."[9]

The *Sky and Water* designs were created right after Escher's work took a dramatic mathematical spin. Escher stepped through what he called the "open gate of mathematics" in 1937. It was then that he read, at his brother's urging, a number of theoretical treatises on crystallography (the science of the form and structure of crystals) and, most significantly, the works of mathematician George Polya. Polya had illustrated 17 specific kinds of symmetrical designs that could be congruently repeated in a plane. While many of these were traditional mosaic or parquet patterns, a number of the motifs had decidedly organic forms, which fit Escher's preference for using "living creatures" within a geometric framework.[10] From 1937 onward, Escher used his considerable graphic art skills to give visual form to uncharted mathematical themes:

> I came to the . . . open gate of mathematics. From there, well-trodden paths lead in every direction, and since then I have often spent time there. Sometimes I think . . . I have trodden all the paths . . . and then I suddenly discover a new path and experience fresh delights.[11]

The regular division of the plane is perhaps the most celebrated of Escher's illustrated mathematical conundrums. He likened the task of illustrating a regular division design to the laying down of black and white linoleum tiles on a flat surface that could, theoretically, extend to infinity. Fitting square tiles snugly together presented the most conventional and rudimentary challenge; octagons, on the other hand, would be more difficult. Thus the more complex the motif, the more challenging and interesting the composition. The evolution of Escher's regular division designs through increasingly complex motifs along a two-dimensional plane can be seen in such works as *Fish* (plate 10), *Verbum* (plate 11), *Regular Division of the Plane with Birds* (plate 23), *Regular Division of the Plane III* (plate 30), and *Regular Division of the Plane V* (plate 31). These two-dimensional studies naturally led to Escher's experimenting with "transitions from the plane to the space," that is, drawing regular division motifs that appear to move from a flat plane to three-dimensionality. The astonishing vision presented in *Reptiles* (plate 13) is an early example of this experimentation, while the evolutionary *Metamorphosis III* (plates 18 and 19), remains the apotheosis of all work with regular division.

Division of the plane was only one of many themes Escher explored in his symmetrical and mathematical designs, but he was never comfortable explaining his work in the esoteric language of science. It was left to mathematician Bruno Ernst (with the artist's full support), to systematically examine and explain the other major themes of Escher's post-1937 work. Besides regular division of the plane, Ernst identified six other ideas that recur throughout the artist's designs: the penetration of worlds, the illusion of space, distorted perspectives, the manipulation of solids and spirals, and the rendering of the "impossible" and the "infinite."[12]

In *Hand with Reflecting Sphere* (plate 7), two different worlds exist in the same place: the artist's "real" hand touches his reflected hand.

In *Magic Mirror* (plate 14), inspired by Lewis Carroll's "Through the Looking-Glass and What Alice Found There," the tiny dragon creatures are "born" from the mirror and those behind it are as "real" as those in front of it.

Escher challenges preconceptions about space in designs like *Day and Night* (plate 6), where the flat planes of the countryside metamorphose into flying geese, and in *Drawing Hands* (plate 17), where each of the three-dimensional "drawing" hands is simultaneously sketching its own "flat" two-dimensional hand.

In *Gallery* (plate 15) and *Relativity* (back cover), Escher distorts perspective to show that technical assumptions about the zenith (the highest vantage point from which to view a scene), the nadir (the lowest vantage point), and distance itself may be only relative concepts. In *Gallery* and *Relativity*, these points are *all* interchangeable. In the even more remarkable *High and Low* (plate 16) and *House of Stairs* (plate 25), Escher uses an invention of his own: curved lines of perspective drawn from the zenith to the nadir. In *High and Low*, "it is not only possible to look down, but also to look down-down." In the *House of Stairs*, "top, bottom, and straight ahead cannot be distinguished" from each other.[13]

Escher's love of crystals and the design possibilities inherent in them is behind the playful motifs in *Concentric Rinds* (plate 20), *Order and Chaos* (plate 21), and *Tetrahedral Planetoid* (plate 24). The use of curved ribbons or stripes, which Escher found so suitable for evoking the sensation of three-dimensionality,[14] are used to arresting effect in *Bond of Union* (plate 29). This serene image of a man and a woman eternally connected was inspired, in part, by H. G. Wells' *The Invisible Man*.

The "impossible" world of the *Print Gallery* (plate 28) suggests that "reality and image are one and the same."[15] A young man who studies a print in the gallery, is in fact a part of the very print he is looking at and can actually see himself as a detail in the picture; at the same time, the viewer of Escher's print also at first only sees a young man looking at a picture. Another "visual pun" is central to the scene depicted in *Ascending and Descending* (plate 32), where the unending ascent and descent of the figures never gets them anywhere; climbing brings them no higher and descending brings them no lower.

One art historian remarked about Escher's body of work that "every one of Escher's plates . . . gives a quintessence, a synthesis of observed reality. . . . And the reality appears to be not only what can be said to have been sensed accurately, but what has been experienced intensely. . . . If necessary, he constructs for himself his own world. There are undoubtedly more people who do this, but not in such an original and efficient way."[16]

Escher lived to see his pioneering work internationally acclaimed and copied over and over again—the ultimate tribute to the graphic artist. He spent the last thirty-two years of his life in Holland, where he died in 1972 at the age of 74.

The mathematical precision and "efficiency" with which Escher designed his prints belied the deeply felt passion he brought to his work, and he was always somewhat perplexed by debates over whether his designs were really "art." On accepting the 1965 Hilversum Culture Prize in Holland, Escher attempted to put the debate to rest: "I try in my prints to testify that we live in a beautiful and orderly world, and not in a formless chaos, as it sometimes seems. . . . To tell you the truth, I find the concept 'art' a bit of a dilemma. What one person calls 'art' is often not 'art' for another. . . . So I am a graphic artist, heart and soul. . . ."[17]

NOTES

1. M. C. Escher, *Escher on Escher: Exploring the Infinite* (New York: Harry N. Abrams, Inc.), 21

2. Doris Schattschneider, *Visions of Symmetry: Notebooks, Periodic Drawings, and Related Work of M. C. Escher* (New York: W. H. Freeman and Company), 15

3. Ibid, 2

4. Ibid, 3

5. Ibid, 5, 7

6. J. L. Locher, Ed., *M. C. Escher: His Life and Complete Graphic Work* (New York: Harry N. Abrams, Inc.), 144

7. Schattschneider, 9–10

8. Locher, 164

9. Escher, 36

10. Schattschneider, 21–23

11. Ibid, 21

12. Locher, 135–154

13. Ibid, 145

14. Escher, 62–63

15. Ibid, 67

16. Schattschneider, 6

17. Escher, 21–22